Sunshine for your Heart

Jordan & Harrison

Sunshine for your Heart
Jordan & Harrison

First published in Australia by Jordan & Harrison 2019

Copyright © Jordan & Harrison 2019
All Rights Reserved

 A catalogue record for this book is available from the National Library of Australia

ISBN: 978-0-6485121-0-3 (pbk)
ISBN: 978-0-6485121-1-0 (ebk)

Typesetting and design by Publicious Book Publishing
Published in collaboration with Publicious Book Publishing
www.publicious.com.au

No part of this book may be reproduced in any form, by photocopying or by any electronic or mechanical means, including information storage or retrieval systems, without permission in writing from both the copyright owner and the publisher of this book.

To all the people who have encouraged, supported,
and inspired us to write this book.

CONTENTS

About the authors	i
Introduction	iii
The shaping of society's thinking	1
How we met	5
Who are you?	9
Are you happy with yourself?	11
Are you happy with the path you have chosen?	16
Are you being true to yourself in this relationship?	19
Being a friend	21
What does love mean to you?	24
Why do we need love?	27
Expressing love	31
Our expressions of love	33
Love is for all shapes and sizes	34
What's the difference between love and lust?	37
Why should it always be about looks?	39
Closeness	41
What is passion?	44
Feelings	45
What is intimacy?	48
Threats to a relationship	51
The need for empathy and compassion	54

Is Marriage the same now as it was in the past?	56
Why are marriages ending in the 20 to 25 year mark?	59
Why do partners stray?	64
What is hurtful to you in your relationship?	67
Can true love exist if one partner wants to control or degrade the other?	69
Why do some women seem to attract selfish and abusive men into their lives?	73
Standing tall and moving forward	76
Internet relationships	79
Why are we together?	81
What keeps us together? / What tears us apart?	84
The need for affection	86
What are signs of affection?	88
Time	91
Time together	94
Spending time together when you have children	96
How can a man make a woman feel good about herself?	98
Our relationship	100
Jordan's view on men	103
Harrison's view on women	104
Thoughts	106
Conclusion	108
References	110
Recommended reading/ DVDS	111

ABOUT THE AUTHORS

Jordan and Harrison are a couple that are both in their second marriage.

They are sharing from their past and present relationships what they have learned along the way to try and offer some ideas for you to help find some Sunshine for your heart as well.

As we contemplated a title for this book, an inspirational thought came to Jordan that perfectly described the very subject that we wanted to write about.

Just as the rays of the sun bring such warmth to our body, so does the experience of true love to our heart

So the title is aptly called: "Sunshine for your heart."

INTRODUCTION

Have you ever wondered why your heart needs sunshine?

It needs it so you can be happy. I'm sure many can relate to this.

When you are unhappy you feel like you down and depressed and nothing seems to be good about your life.

In contrast when everything seems to be going great, you feel like you are on top of the world and you feel happy.

It is a known fact that the more positivity in your life the stronger you become, your energy increases, and your health improves, which in may help your life be prolonged

While we hear so much talk about the need to look after our physical heart, that wonderful organ that sits inside our chest and pumps the blood through our body, there is another heart we need to take care of.

Your emotional heart needs to be healthy because if this is so, you have the will to live and there is a desire to see your value and to look after yourself.

It is a very sad reality that today many people have had some sad emotional experiences. Life has become very painful to them due to failed relationships.

Some may have as a result been walking in gloomy darkness, fearing to take the risk of attempting to find that ideal life partner due to some, emotion trauma they have gone through, but we want to give you hope and encouragement.

Anything is possible no matter what your traumatic past that may have left you feeling so low such as coming from an experience of constantly been told by the cold, cruel lips of your ex-partner that no one would ever want you.

It is certainly time like never before that individuals need brightness brought back into their lives. That is the purpose of this book.

It is written in a way that hopefully many can relate to, and we trust that all who read it will be greatly inspired and not give up in discouragement no matter your past or present circumstance.

The content of this book has been designed to include variety of information and helpful quotes for different readers, young and old who are individually looking for the answers they seek for.

It also includes some of the practical experiences that we have and are constantly applying to our lives to keep our love strong.

Enjoy what you read, as it comes from our heart to yours as a gift to be exactly what the title suggests "Sunshine for your heart."

Remember sunshine not only brings warmth but also dispels the darkness and in the context of this book the darkness is ignorance and error, two things that can prevent us from experiencing the very best.

Jordan & Harrison

MAYBE

"Maybe we were supposed to meet the wrong people before meeting the right one, so that when we finally meet the right person, we will know how to be grateful for that gift.

Maybe when the door of happiness closes, another opens: but often times, we look at the closed door that we don't even see the new one that has been open for us.

Maybe it is true that e don't know what we have until we lose it, but is also true but we don't know what we have been missing until it arrives.

Maybe the happiest of people don't necessary have the best of everything: they just make the most of everything that comes along their way.

Maybe the brightest future will be based on a forgotten past: after all, you can't go on successfully in life until you let go of your past mistakes, failures and heartaches.

Maybe the best kind of friend is the kind you can sit on a porch and swing with, never say a word, and then walk away feeling like it was the best conversation you've ever had.

Maybe you shouldn't go for looks; they can deceive; don't go for wealth; even that fades away.

Go for someone who makes you smile, because it takes only a smile to make a dark day bright.

Find the one that makes your heart smile."

Anonymous

1: THE SHAPING OF SOCIETY'S THINKING

Harrison says:
All over this world there are many different cultures, customs and traditions. What is passed down to each of us has in many cases been the result of the teachings and way of life for many of our former ancestors.

What I am about to express is based on my experience in living in a western country, which in my case was Australia.

There is no doubt that from a young age we are conditioned to think and act a certain way, usually due to a variety of early influences that tend to shape our thinking. For many, there are many contributing factors that tend to do this.

There is the example of our parents in and out of the home is in a way a model of the way that a man and a woman are meant to be towards each other by the way they communicate and hopefully by the way emotional love is shown.

Of course there is also the education we gain in the classroom, and schoolyard, from well-meaning teachers and deceived peers sincerely thinking they have all the answers.

On top of this, there is the strong influence of the entertainment world with its various movies, sports, and current music styles and their corresponding suggestive lyrics.

There is a newer element that the young people of today have to contend with the increase of technology in the form of social media via the internet and mobile phones which brings all sorts of images and false ideals to their developing minds.

The combination of all these factors have an impact on many resulting in fake realties about life, leading to, in many cases immoral attitudes and actions.

Males, for example, can be conditioned to think manliness is to be aggressive and to look upon females only in a sexual way. To be convinced that someone is attractive only if their face and body looks nice.

As a result, a brainwashed and sensual breed of young and even, older men fail to see what true beauty is. So called beautiful women are thought of as only those who are slim and well proportioned. One that they regard as looking hot.

Sadly, not only men but also women buy into this lie by their actions and this is shown, in one example by the way they dress, especially when going out to nightclubs, even on the coldest of nights with hardly any clothes on.

This is tragic because these females help feed the lustful passions of the men who they are on display to.

They are also placing themselves at risk both from sexual predators and also to their health because of the exposure to the cool air on those areas of their bodies that should be covered up such as legs, arms and chest.

The sad fact also is that women who do not fall into that beautiful category feel that they are ugly and not worth having someone to love and value them for who they really are.

The truth of the matter is, it is not merely the way someone looks that makes them beautiful but the person within who longs to reveal their true self not being fake, but as a genuine loving expression of life.

I believe that part of the result of the shaping of society is that looks are all that count, but by way of contrast it is in my opinion that these questions should be asked:

Are looks always important, or is the character and values that the person stands for vital as well?

Have I allowed myself to be swayed by false ideals instead of seeing what true attractiveness is, which is beyond mere external qualities?

Have I felt that the so called beautiful and handsome people in this world are only worthy of love and affection?

These are questions worth considering, for many have been deceived by modern societies thinking which has in many ways been distorted and shaped as the title of this chapter suggests by the various influences that we have around and before us.

Remember though that as individuals, couples and families it does not have to continue in our life this way.

For so long, I thought that if I did not measure up to the way someone else looked or behaved I was a nothing and definitely not worth loving!

How sad that so many of us do not see how unique we all are because of a negative and false mindset we hold onto.

Jordan says:

Society is a group of people that come together. So this group of people can cause chains of events to occur in the forms of judgements of the human race.

They can perceive to change the thinking and treatment of other human beings in the form of clothing, style and fashion, health and the food that we choose to consume, whether good or bad for us, the people that we choose to be friend or love, and the list goes on.

Why do we let others make our choices for us? This is our life so why are we not the ones making the choices?

Don't we suffer the consequences for our own actions? So then why are we not making the decisions that may be mistakes or not, but they are ours to make.

Yet if someone else sways us, to their way of thinking and we too make that choice because of a peer pressure type of decision, they are not the ones suffering the consequence we are. If it means we need to stand alone for the choice that we want amongst a pack, then what is stopping us?

We either want what we want or we want what everyone else wants, and by doing that we lose our individuality, our own decision making, and in some cases our identity.

> 'Remember, no amount of physical beauty
> will ever be as valuable as a beautiful heart.'

Power of positivity

2: HOW WE MET

Harrison says:
Jordan and I met at an over 35's social dance club. During that time of our initial meeting we both felt very comfortable with each other as we talked and danced.

Having quite a few things in common with someone is always refreshing and that was what we discovered as we covered various topics about our lives and interests.

My main recollection of that event was that I remember thinking that it was like Jordan and I had known each other for a long time, because of the way in which we connected.

As both of us got to know the other more when we had time together over the next few weeks, we found a very strong friendship develop that was fast growing into a deep and strong love.

It was a wonderful experience spending a lot of quality time together, as we knew that we had a unique connection, something that rarely happens between people.

It was and is real. Soul mates is probably the best way to describe it. Two individuals not afraid to be themselves, truly loving and not being ashamed of showing it. This was demonstrated then and it has been continued in the things we have done and are doing together.

Whether it be dancing, talking, driving in a car together the same principles have always been there, that is to give one hundred per cent of each other to each other.

Admittedly, it had been a risk for either of us to attempt something serious again for there were within us scars of two broken hearts that were the results of a failed relationship.

There was a time of healing for both of us, but despite this fact we chose to make a go of it. One of the main issues we had to face was that we knew there would be a certain of emotional baggage to deal with.

In spite of this fact we also sensed that there would be a mutual support from each other. This gave us both an assurance that we had someone in our lives who understood and with enough love to go through it together and grow regardless of our past.

We both knew deep down there had to be something better than what we had experienced in our previous relationships, and I say this not too be too critical against our former spouses.

While I guess that can be excused to a point, there comes a time in everyone's life when a crisis comes, a moment when it hits home to the heart that thing need to change.

As was inevitable, not everyone liked the fact that Jordan and I had met and enjoyed each other's company, but jealousy and envy can revel itself in many ways.

Jordan recalled how one night while using the toilet at one of the dance clubs we used to go a lot on a Sunday night she overheard a couple of ladies expressing their displeasure over the fact Harrison was with her? Something they could not understand.

I knew exactly why I was with her then and why I am with her now. I am so thankful to have met

Jordan and I can now say, without a doubt that I am richly enjoying the gift and experience of a wonderful relationship, lived out within the sacred institution of marriage, the way it was originally intended.

When one finds what he or she has always been looking for in the ideal person and a strong relationship naturally results, then it should be embraced with open arms with a sheer determination never to let it go.

Jordan says:

I remember the night like it was yesterday. It was February 11, 2009 at a club in Melbourne. I was sitting at a table there, talking with my friend Glenys when I noticed this kind and handsome looking man walk in and smile as he was greeted by the lady at the door.

He then paid the entry fee and made his way along in front of the bar counter area to a seat where he sat down by himself. After a while he approached Glenys and after saying hello asked her if she would like to dance.

She declined but said I might like to, so he asked me. Of course I said yes. This was the beginning of me meeting this kind looking man. He said his name was Harrison and he helped me out of my chair we then headed for the dance floor.

I like to dance so I was happy to have said yes. We reached the dance floor and not knowing each other we did the dancing pose of 10 feet apart. We talked while we danced and was still dancing and talking even after the music had stopped, and found that we had a lot in common.

We continued the conversation for most of the night there from the dance floor to table 18. That night and my meeting Harrison was to change the rest of my life, more than I ever dreamed it would. From that night I became really alive, which enabled me to be truly myself.

I no longer had to pretend to be who I wasn't in order to fit in, as I had done for the past 23 years in my previous relationship. I didn't know what the future had in store for me, but I felt comfortable and safe with Harrison and hoped we would be together.

A few weeks before I met Harrison I had prayed to God asking him to please bring someone into my life who would love me just for me, and he did.

There is no doubt in both our minds that we are together because of him, and that he has big things in store for us, so let's see what is ahead for us shall we?

3: WHO ARE YOU?

Harrison says:
Who am I? This is a question that all of us at one time or another ask ourselves. The search for our unique identity can be realized earlier or later in life depending on each person.

For me, it took many years of not truly being who I was made to be because of a combination of low self-worth and trying to fit into the false identity that I thought I was supposed to be.

This is not an uncommon thing I am sure in many lives as they lose their way in this, at times confusing world. Who am you is something that we each, in the quietness of our own mind at one time or another needs to answer.

What do you answer in your own mind, reader in response to that age old question? Be honest, do you see yourself as an insignificant product of chance or a miracle of creation that has been given special ability and a personality unique to only you.

Jordan says:
Here are some questions that I have been asking myself. Maybe these can help you as well.

Do you know who you really are? Do you know what your purpose for your life is? Do you know what you want out of your life?

Do you know what your goals and dreams are? Are you doing anything about them? If not. Why not?

Are you happy with your life? Are you happy being the person that you are on the inside?

Can you give more to others? Do you do anything for others? What makes you happy? Are you doing what makes you happy? If no then why not?

What do you want from a relationship? What do you expect from your partner? I could go on and on but you can write your own questions and answer them.

Everyone is different so the questions and the answers will be different too. I guess in my last relationship I had an identity crisis because I was pretending to be someone that I was not in order to fit in with everyone.

I let them use me to fit in and in the end this is still affecting me in my current relationship. Sometimes we pretend to be strong like a lion yet underneath we are really a teddy bear.

I let things get to me because I am a caring person and that affects me deeply. I know who I am and I am now that person I was again before I met my previous husband and his family.

I know what I want from my life and I have a plan of what I want to do to achieve it. The question now is can I make it happen being me? I am going to give it my best shot starting with completing and publishing this book.

4: ARE YOU HAPPY WITH YOURSELF?

Harrison says:
When it comes to relationships, it is essential that we also have a healthy acceptance of ourselves.

It is very important that we are really happy as an individual, that is, the way we look, our personality, values and abilities that we all have been gifted with.

It is very sad that many of us can go through life and never discover who we really are. Why do we have to compare ourselves with others when we each have something special to offer?

We somehow think that we ought to behave like this person or that person to either be accepted by others or even ourselves. To fit into someone else's ideal is simply living a lie, and deep down, if we are really honest, hopefully we will eventually realize that.

This can result from the numerous expectations of the world's ideals of cliché's, expectations and social roles. Now, what exactly do I mean by that?

Think about this for a minute, are we really being our genuine selves when mixing with our family, friends and work associates or are we just living out a script that the social structures around us have molded us to be?

It's a trap many of us can fall into so easily. It takes courage to be true in a world that is ever trying to take that right away from us.

Certainly, while there may be times to admire those positive traits in certain successful people that you may regard as a good role model because of their achievements this should not stop us from appreciating who we are and the potential we have.

It is not a shameful thing to shine as our true selves, so why not give ourselves permission to do so. Not only are we to admire the special qualities in each other but also to appreciate our individual uniqueness as a human being who has a place and a purpose in this life.

I believe that we need to stop and reflect on who we are, what we have to offer, and then develop every part of our being through the wisdom and strength of our Maker, because then we can become living, loving, giving individuals.

There are various elements and forces out there that are determined to try get you to think you are not that valuable. One is bullying that occurs in various forms, from the child's school ground, via the internet's social sites and even adults in the workplace, and in our everyday life.

Either way, wherever, however and whenever this bullying has occurred, it still has a very damaging effect on victims involved, causing them to question their sense of worth and identity.

Perhaps you, dear reader have gone through some experience when you felt unworthy of betterment. Maybe you had someone in your life who really thought that you would amount to nothing or that the talents you had were not worth using.

How sad it is that we believe these lies which keep us down for years- but the truth can set us free. Don't let anyone hold you back. Be courageous to let go of the past. Let go of false ideas told you by Jealous, cruel, fake and insecure people.

You have the right move forward as the true you, even though it may feel strange at first. I personally believe that deep within our very being, there is something waiting to come out and reveal itself in its fullness.

We often hear this term as developing and reaching our full potential. Each has something special to offer in this life, may it never be wasted as you develop your true self.

I believe that as one makes the choice to be in a relationship, remember that the ideal person to be with is someone who will help you enhance the individual you already are.

Sadly enough, I have seen some people who choose to stay in a relationship because of the low opinion they have on themselves and therefore do not think that is not worth choosing a better life.

Certain partners in this style of relationships sense their control over the other party in cases like this, and therefore make every opportunity to tell them they are nothing and that no one else would want them either.

Maybe you have been in that situation or perhaps you have known someone who for years has been made to feel like a second class citizen.

It is heartbreaking to see or experience it, that is for sure, but as I stated before, remember who you are, no matter what anyone out of spite, jealousy or simply down right selfish cruelty has said or done.

Jordan says:

I have found that to truly be happy with yourself means firstly not to compare who you are with others. Secondly, accept the unique way you are, but in my case I find it easier to say than do.

That means all your abilities, your looks and the personality that you have been gifted with. Once you have come to this point in your experience, then realize that you can develop into your very best.

'Are you happy with yourself?', this is a question that can go in all different directions as there is so much to think about before you can answer.

For me, there is how you look, feel, my choices, is my life fulfilling? Am I doing what I am passionate about? If I was to answer this right now it would be no. Why?

I am not happy with how I look or feel as I was told by my ex for 23 years that I was big, fat and ugly. He also said no one else would want me which made me feel worthless and bad about myself.

My husband now tells me numerously everyday he loves me and calls me beautiful. He also cuddles and kisses me which is definitely, the opposite to what I had been used to. My passion is to help people however I can.

I have been doing this in the form of money, food and gifts-everything I can to whoever needs it with what we can afford. I am glad my husband shares this passion too.

I am not happy with how I feel because of injuries that cause me chronic pain 24/7 but I soldier on to do what I can.

For me to be truly happy with myself I would need a lot of things and circumstances to change but I plod along the best I can and cope with what I have been given. One day I hope to say to say my answer with be yes.

> 'Our deepest fear is not that we are inadequate.
>
> Our deepest fear is that we are powerful beyond measure.
>
> It is our light, not our darkness that most frightens us.
>
> We ask ourselves, who am I to be brilliant, gorgeous, talented, and fabulous?
>
> Actually, who are you not to be?
>
> As we let our own light shine, we unconsciously give other people permission to do the same.
>
> As we are liberated from our own fear, our presence automatically liberates others'
>
> *Marianne Williamson*

5: ARE YOU HAPPY WITH THE PATH YOU HAVE CHOSEN?

Harrison says:
Sometimes it may take many years of suffering and disappointment before we realize that the path we have chosen may not be doing us any good.

Of course once we come to this realization, perhaps we need to look for a better way to live. For example, if your health is poor, a wise thing to do would be to look to the cause, which may include a healthier eating, exercising and resting plan.

The same goes with failed relationships, it's important to ask oneself what keeps going wrong and why. Is the fault in me, is there some area I need to work on.

So find out how to make a new start, begin again on a path that will bring better results with less pain. Be encouraged, it is never too late to change. A lot of material is out there to educate you on this subject.

To alter the way of thinking and doing things is not a popular or comfortable idea for some people especially when they have this crazy prideful notion that they are doing nothing wrong.

After all who likes being told that a lot of habits and beliefs they have lived out for so many years is most likely going to cause them to experience heartache, disappointment and sadness?

If a lot of people your age are doing nothing to improve their health or other significant areas in their lives including their relationships that do not mean the concepts within this book are strange or even wrong- it simply says that most people will find it difficult to stand alone and be different from the crowd.

Jordan says:
This is a good question for you to ask yourself right now. So are you?

Paths change all the time for one reason or another, and you should not be afraid to change it. To change it could be for the better, but it could also change for the worst but in saying that you will never know if you don't give it a go.

I have been afraid most of my life of one thing or another and way too scared to change most things in my life that I wanted to and dreamed of, as not to rock the boat as the saying goes but I am finding now as I am getting older if I don't then I will never know.

My path in my 54 years has changed. When you are young you always say I want to be ___when I grow up. This usually follows with nurse, fireman, a policeman etc. I'm sure we have all done that.

I always wanted my career choice to be a nurse because I love to help people and always have. When I am a patient in the hospital I find myself helping the other patients in my room, if I can.

I have had many career changes over the years, plus I always wanted a family of my own. I had an accident when I was younger and was told I may not be able to have children.

To my surprise and joy I had 3 children of my own plus I took on step and foster children as well. Family is the most important people to me, no matter what.

My chosen path has been to be a wife and mother first. I was this for 23 years, but because of circumstances my path changed again. My path now is a happier but still a challenging one because of injury and financial circumstances.

I have a lot of dreams that I would like to see become real because they are all about helping others, but there is a lot involved to make these happen. I hope in the near future to say yes, I am happy with my chosen path.

I know that God made me with a kind caring heart to do good things for others, to be a good mother and family orientated woman, and I try my best to be this. I know in my heart that in the future things will happen because I will make them. Just remember none of us are perfect. We are human and as humans we all make mistakes no matter who we are, and this means if at first you don't succeed, please keep trying.

Frustration often steers you to the right path.

Joyce Rachelle

6: ARE YOU BEING TRUE TO YOURSELF IN THIS RELATIONSHIP?

Harrison says:
It is very important to be honest about your relationship. True satisfaction is found in also making someone else happy but nevertheless there should be some kind of harmony and growth between you and your partner otherwise, is there any point being together?

Another thing to consider is this. Can you truly be yourself in this relationship or do you find that you are trying to be someone false just to please the one you are with?

I was in little ways doing that in my previous marriage not only to fit in to a role I was pretending to play both in the presence of my first wife and in laws. To be trying to live out not who you really are but someone's expectations of how you should be is not freedom and definitely not love.

If you, dear reader have been or are currently in such a predicament it may be time to examine your situation and to hopefully find that solution, firstly by being true to yourself then to rebuild on a better foundation within your relationship that both involves openness and perhaps even change.

Jordan says:

Questions to consider: Are you happy in your relationship? Are you getting from your relationship what you should be? What should I be getting you ask?

Something that may be worthwhile doing is to sit down with a cuppa, a pen and writing paper and with a relaxed and honest state of mind simply question yourself.

Think about your current relationship using the following headings:

Why am I in this relationship? What do I give to this relationship? What am I getting from this relationship?

How important is my true happiness to me? Am I in a rut, doing the same things because it's comfortable –even if I'm unhappy? Well what are you going to do about it? Are you living YOUR life for others?

So many more questions for asking once you get thinking about it all. I can honestly say that in my relationship with Harrison, I am giving him my all because I love him with all my heart. He is my whole world.

There are no expectations. We are individuals, but I feel like we are from the same mold, just a male and a female version of the same person.

We are so much alike and have so much in common that he makes it easy for me to be me and gives me the freedom to be true to myself in this wonderful loving relationship we have.

7: BEING A FRIEND

Harrison says:
Friendship, what is it to you? There may be many definitions to what being a friend is all about, and today we often need reminding of what that word really means.

While pondering this subject, there are a few questions to prompt your thinking. Is friendship being a companion who stands by another person even when others don't?

Is it something that you are willing to hold on to? That friend, no matter the cost, and does it demonstrate loyalty, showing that you can be trusted when your friend confides in you?

Is it something you never stop being while reaching out and being a true friend through good times and bad? Sadly, the word friend just like the word love has been cheapened today.

On social media, for example you have friends you can add on your contact list, but in many cases these names are merely acquaintances.

There are some exceptions of course. Being a friend also means respecting when someone wants to be just that. What do I mean by that? I will give a scenario to illustrate my point.

I know someone who has accepted the friendship of someone of the opposite sex who while this man has been helpful to her in many ways by way of companionship and assisting her with manual tasks she does not want to be romantically involved with him.

He on the other hand wants the opposite and has many times expressed to her how he feels. He has even recently let her know that he does not want to see her with any other man.

This is not friendship in the true sense but straight out possessiveness, a trait of character that is wrong because it claims ownership on another person at the expense of their freedom.

Understandably the woman I am writing about had to cut ties with this male friend. There may be potential problems when being a friend to someone of the opposite sex as you go through experiences together which brings a depth to that friendship.

That doesn't mean that friendships can't develops into a strong loving relationship, the example of what happened between Jordan and I proves that this can occur.

I believe that it really depends on how far you want the friendship to go, and what mutual boundaries you have.

Most importantly, I believe that a good strong friendship can be enduring when it's correct and respectful principles are always adhered to.

Jordan says:

In my experience being a friend is important because you get to know that person, share good and bad things that happen to both of you and your friendship grows and you go from there.

When I met Harrison, we became friends, we went to the movies, had meals together and went dancing. We found we could confide in each other about everything.

We talked for hours together and still do about all sorts of topics. Our friendship remains with us and always will be. Friendship is a solid basis to a good relationship, and Harrison is my best friend.

I never really had friends in my life time so I cannot really comment on any other friendship than my friendship with my husband.

I can say however that I have seen others friendships over the years and been jealous of some of them, especially when things take a turn for the worst, that's when you know who your true friends are.

I never really had anyone. The man who were supposed to be my husband for the 23 years of my previous marriage, well it was the loneliest time of my life.

He didn't stand up for me against his family or do anything a good true friend would do for another one.

Rare as is true love, true friendship is rarer.

Jean de La Fontaine

8: WHAT DOES LOVE MEAN TO YOU?

Harrison says:
Love, what is it all about? As you know, there have been so many definitions of it, of course there are some more accurate than others.

So what does love mean to you? Would you regard it a fuzzy feeling, or having the contented experience of gazing into each other's eyes and simply being in love? Whatever your idea of what it is all about, many authors and experts have agreed that love has many aspects.

A lot of research has been written and sung about it over the centuries and decades, so we ask the question to you, the reader of this book, who perhaps is someone seeking to understand the true meaning of this eternal theme, what does love mean to you?

As you ponder the answer to this timely question take serious note of the following words. You were born to have the potential for growth and development in every area of your life, yes including being able to give and receive true emotional love. So, what is love?

From our personal research and experience, we have discovered that true love is not always based on a happy flight of feeling, or even infatuation, but a strong enduring principle that always seeks the highest wellbeing of the person you claim to love.

It is my opinion that true love is often expressed not only in words but in action as well. So the motivation that one has is not selfish but to totally give of oneself to another to uplift, cherish and give value to their beloved.

One who seeks only what he or she can get out of a relationship does not know what love is all about. That is no more than disguised selfishness. Love that is true is indeed a most wonderful thing to experience.

It goes beyond the externals of saying how beautiful or handsome someone is, but has greater depth and is willing to endure all sorts of trials, and still remain true.

Is love something that is not as strong as it used to be, or is it possible that other things have simply taken a higher priority?

If you feel there is no hope, don't stress, be thankful that even in the midst of a period in this world's history when the statistics of broken marriages and failed relationships are everywhere, you don't necessarily have to go down that same path.

Jordan says:

This is a question to me that has many answers. I have asked this question to numerous individuals over the years.

The responses I got ranged from silly looks, especially on men's faces to the look of I want to be loved on female's faces. My ex-husband, when I asked him what does love mean to you?

Looked at me silly then responded with, I don't know what love is. I thought afterward from the upbringing he came from, I was not surprised by his answer.

I guess it is the case of monkey see monkey do, and in that situation the father monkey did not show any kind of love to the mother monkey, so my ex-husband had no idea.

When you are shown love, surveys have proved you are happy, less stressed, more content and you live longer.

My husband shows me love every day, in one form or another and it makes me happy to know I am unconditionally and truly loved no matter what just for being me.

He loves me for my inside heart and my outside looks, but I don't agree with him about the outside because I hate how I look.

Love to me in my current relationship is happiness, caring, kindness, smiling, laughing, crying, basically being able to do all of these things and still have my husband standing by me no matter what.

To be able to say what I think, how I am feeling, or have a bad day, and I can honestly say that these things have happened with no judgement only support and love. I am very lucky.

> **"You don't love someone for their looks, or their clothes or for their fancy car, but because they sing a song only you can hear."**
>
> *Oscar Wilde.*

9: WHY DO WE NEED LOVE?

Harrison says:
Deep down I have always wanted to experience both the giving and receiving of true and genuine love-something that I have noticed is hard to come by in a world that in some ways has become very cold and loveless.

To be loved helps you see your worth through someone else's eyes, by what they say and what they do, I could not agree more.

I need love to help me grow and be that person that I was created for. When I have someone near me, loving and encouraging me in spite of my failings, it helps me get up and keep going.

It is in the secure knowledge of being in a relationship where love is freely received and freely given that I can be myself without being criticized unnecessarily because I have not met someone's expectations.

Sadly I have in the past been in a relationship where, to be honest the love that I have just described was not experienced. There may have been at the beginning some aspects of emotional closeness that may be termed love but when the testing time of life's pressures and stresses came then that love oh so quickly transformed into the negativity of coldness and fear.

Why do I need love? I have known life without it and it does not sit comfortable with me. To truly love is to truly live it is in such an environment that my wife and I are complete.

How you answer this question is up to you, but personally, as I have already stated, I need love to help me realize my value. It also inspires me for growth and development as the emotional part of me is deeply fulfilled.

Whether we accept this thought or not, we cannot deny the fact that we were meant to love and be loved. As we all know, life can be very lonely without someone there for us who truly loves us for who we are. The precious thing we call love is something that helps make life worth living.

Without love in our life, we are not complete. Have you ever wondered what this world would be without love? I am sure you agree it would be a very dark place.

We take this for granted don't we and though there have been times in this world's violent history when individuals and groups of people have displayed utter hatred towards others this still does not discount the eternal truth that we were originally created to love and be loved.

Jordan says:
The reason I need love is to make me feel appreciated, wanted and needed. To be loved by Harrison makes me feel happy. To know that he loves me with everything he has unconditionally is worth more than winning tattslotto.

To me, nothing is more precious than your health, your happiness and to be loved by someone with all their heart. With the knowledge to know that I am loved makes me shine like a bright star in the sky. It's like I am glowing with love for him, just as he is for me.

When you feel loved it changes your outlook on everything. It has mine. It makes you stop and reflect about what your life was before experiencing true love.

When I really think about it, like so many people, I personally had not had love in my life before and so I did not know how it felt or what to expect.

Now, I am thankful that I can wake up everyday hearing Harrison tells me that he loves me. It is so good to hear these words not only at the beginning of the day but also at the end of it as he tells me the same thing before I go to sleep. Harrison not only tells me but shows me in many ways as well that I am loved. To be loved is to know that I am of value to someone and with a conscious sense of that knowledge I have worth.

My heart feels warm and happy like the rays of sunshine that shine on us on a beautiful day, hence sunshine for your heart. I was asked one day could I see myself not loving Harrison. My answer was will the sun stop shining?

I wish everyone could experience the true real genuine love from a partner. Other than the miracle of life it is the most amazing feeling.

I hope that all our children get to experience this for themselves.

To me, love is an expression of many things to someone who means the world to you, or who makes you feel like you would lay down your life for them, or trust your life to them.

To your husband, partner, best friend, companion or even your own family. I personally need to be shown and know that my family especially love and care. Family is everything to me.

For my husband to love me by showing this in word and action makes my heart smile. Intimacy is a very big deal to some people, and hard for them to show.

I find it hard because of how I was made feel from my previous relationship. I am starting to feel a bit more comfortable showing Harrison intimacy but it has taken a lot of years to feel ok about doing that.

He does this every day for he is the one who knows me better than I do myself. My husband now can tell you everything about me. For example what is my favorite colour, music or movie?

Sadly, by way on contrast, my ex-husband could not tell you one thing such as has been mentioned, about me which showed he did not really care.

10: EXPRESSING LOVE

Harrison says:
I have come to realise that to tell someone you love them is not always enough. If love is not shown in action as well, to say I love you is merely words. I am thankful that I am with someone who loves to give and receive the various expressions of love I delight to do.

The different expressions of love range from a loving hug, a foot rub, an encouraging word or doing something simply like carrying in the groceries from the car to the kitchen.

I did not see too much expression of love between my parents or grandparents that are not to the level that I think should be but that may be a combination of the generation and personality types.

It may have been the same with you, dear reader but that does not mean you have to follow their example. If you really want to have a rich, love filled relationship you do not need to be afraid to express it to the fullest.

Jordan says:
I express what I believe to be my way of feeling love by looking lovingly at my husband. Holding him and telling him why I love him. Some people find it really hard to express love, let alone what love means to them. Love can mean many things.

To some people it means nothing at all Women think it's only men that have problems expressing their feelings, but it's not, some women have difficulty doing that as well.

It is not something to be ashamed of. A lot of people never saw affection being expressed in their family upbringing so they have no idea how to either.

In my own family's upbringing I saw a little bit of affection in my parent's relationship but none in my grandparents, so I wonder why I am the so called "black sheep" of the family because I want to receive and give affection. Having Harrison express his love for me is an amazing feeling.

To experience the special emotion of having someone actually loving me for me, with my large body and all is a miracle to me. For so long I did not feel I deserved to be loved because I had for 23 years of being told how big, fat and ugly I was.

It is taking a long time for me to feel that it is ok for me to feel deserving of someone loving me.

11: OUR EXPRESSIONS OF LOVE

One way to show love is by words of appreciation expressed freely, either written or spoken of and to the one you love. Here are some examples that we have both written to each other in cards and from our thoughts book that we compiled.

Thank you Jordan for the gift of yourself.
 I love you xxoo

Every hour of every day I think about you, and us, and our life together, the past, the present, and what is before us. I know we will be happier than we are now as a result of our relationship, our communication our love, and our openness.
 We will always be there for each other, no matter what. Our love is a very special love that no one else can experience except us, my husband and I. xxoo.

Today is our 6 month anniversary. I am so more in love with you Harrison as I was when I first met you. When I look into your eyes, I see a vast difference to the first time. You are so much happier and content since I came into your life, just as I am because of you. I will love you forever xoxo.

12: LOVE IS FOR ALL SHAPES AND SIZES

Harrison says:
I know that Jordan has had a few issues about how she looks since we met even though I tell her over and over again that to me she is beautiful both within and without.

To be honest as well I at times have had a bit of a body image. At the time of our initially meeting I was quite thin and scrawny with a couple of missing teeth which I was very self-conscious of.

Since then although my missing teeth have been replaced with dentures, I have some extra gray hair, a bald patch. This combined with my skinny arms and legs have been a bother- but this is me.

Our experience proves it that, in spite of the so-called physical defects we saw in ourselves, we both found someone who loved and accepted us. If you feel that because you are a certain shape or size no-one would love you then, think again. I believe that there is someone out there for everyone.

Jordan says:
Why it is some people think that love can only be for skinny, attractive people? Larger people need love too and I think there is someone for everyone.

Everyone deserves to have someone to love and to love them unless they decide that's not what they want in their life. I dreamed of someone to truly love and who would truly love me.

I waited till I was 44 to find him. The point being, I did find him. I have read about people finding love and marrying at 75 years of age, maybe even older, so what!

I'm a large lady and I have someone to love me, so why can't others to of all shapes and sizes have someone to love? If you want it, it will come to you when the time is right.

I didn't go looking for Harrison but he found me as he was looking for a lifelong love just as I was.

What people don't think about when they are looking is, don't go at it like a bull at a gate so to speak because if it's supposed to be it will happen naturally.

Something else people don't consider about larger people is why they are that size. They just assume that they are that size because they eat junk food all day, but in my case, it's a medical problem.

As far as my diet is concerned, I eat quite healthy I eat approximately 85% raw food, having a good amount of fruit and vegetables.

People can be cruel when they judge me without knowing my condition or what I am going through. I hate it when they are looking at you that you know what they are thinking. It's hurtful.

Don't you think I want to be thin, pretty and gorgeous like all the models you see on the T.V and in the magazines, well I do. I also think about what these pictures must be doing to women and young girls today. Basically, they assaying you have to starve yourself to be like that.

Anorexia Nervosa is not a pretty sight. Have you ever seen anyone with that disease? Maybe you should. Men can get it as well, it's not only women that have hang-ups about their appearance.

Men have feelings too as some of us tend to forget. People are of the opinion that women only suffer from anorexia but they are wrong. I am not sure of the percentage of men, but I am sure it would show a reasonable amount.

Men tend not to show their feelings and problems or talk to anyone about them, so how would you know? Couples come in all shapes and sizes. Some are happy, some are not.

It all boils down to what size and shape you are happy to live with in a death do us part relationship, without wanting to be with a different one after a while.

13: WHAT IS THE DIFFERENCE BETWEEN LOVE AND LUST?

Harrison says:

From my own personal experience in relationships, the difference between love and lust is that lust is primarily a self-centered passion that comes and goes relying on feelings and is motivated by self-gratification.

It does not stop to consider consequences of behavior and usually relies on merely the physical attributes of another person. I believe that true love thinks of the other person's needs, it displays a self-sacrificing attitude that is willing to go through a trial such as a financial or a health crisis together.

It does not rely on feelings merely but on a heavenly inspired principle which remembers the words of the Holy Scripture that says, love suffers long and is kind and that it bears all things, believes all things, hopes all things and endures all things. It holds on to the words which declare love never fails.

(1 Corinthians 13:4, 7, 8)

Jordan says:

I have found the lust thing happened for me when I was young in my twenties. I think we all go through it one way or another. It's usually lusting after a T.V star or a famous personality. I haven't met anyone yet who never did it. It's usually just sexual.

Love, for me is a feeling of wanting to be with that special person forever, it feel like your hearts aching when that person isn't around.

Lust on the other hand is based on sensual feelings that come and go, it can fall into the same category as being infatuated with someone, or perhaps thinking about sexual things concerning that person you may have either looked at or merely had a brief exchanged of words at a social gathering, a nightclub or even at work.

By contrast, love is deep, it is lasting. It is not based on feelings or appearances alone, but on the whole person whose company you delight to be in. The way they talk, the values they stand for.

> "True Love is not a strong, fiery impetuous passion.
>
> On the contrary, it is calm and deep in it's nature.
>
> It looks beyond mere externals, and is attracted by qualities alone.
>
> It is wise and discriminating, and its devotion is real and abiding".
>
> *E.G White.*

14: WHY SHOULD IT BE ABOUT THE WAY WE LOOK?

Harrison says:
A lot of us are programed to think and act a certain way from the example of others and what the media portray. How do we define who is beautiful and who is not?

To me, it's someone who has a warm loving personality, someone who will stand by you as trustworthy and someone who is not afraid to express their true self as one of God's marvels of creation.

So, what if they do not have that so called perfect face, hair or body? Those things are outward merely but true beauty comes from within and it shines through.

We don't have to look too far, only at the local supermarkets checkouts or news agency to see displayed those glossy magazines that portray the men, women and sadly even children that are actors, actresses or the latest music performer.

So many men and women, boys and girls see their faces and bodies displayed before them and at times feel so inadequate compared to their stars or idols. This feeling of inadequacy or inferiority that one holds on to can hinder our personal development and prevent us being the best we can be in a loving relationship.

We are all unique, all special and have the potential of doing much good in an unselfish way by connecting with another person who longs to express the same thing.

Jordan says:

In my 54 years of life I have noticed a lot of things when Harrison and I walk through the shopping centres. I watch the women look at him as they approach us and the men as well look at me. It is natural for men to look at women and visa-versa.

Harrison is now aware of it as he wasn't before, and he too watches the responses. For some reason, most men seem to want a partner who is slim, has long hair, big breasts and beautiful.

Well, I am here to tell you I would like to be all those too, but here is my real world, it will never be. Why is that? Because not all women are thin beautiful and big breasted.

In the real world both men and women are all different shapes and sizes. What happened to what's on the inside is what counts? That is how I was brought up, to get to know the heart of a person then their looks. The real part of a person is their heart and what it feels. If you get someone like that it's a win.

15: CLOSENESS

Harrison says:
From my understanding the term, closeness is similar in definition to intimacy and one cannot really exist without the other. I firmly believe that closeness between two people is possible although for some who are not used to it, the thought of being not only physically but also emotionally close to someone can be a bit frightening.

I know that each person who enters into a relationship with another has a certain amount of what is called baggage. They may have come from an abusive relationship, had some kind of childhood trauma, not seen real closeness between their parents or they simply have felt more comfortable distancing themselves from others.

Anything new can feel awkward at first, but this does not mean it is wrong if it is in harmony with right principles that can only enhance a loving relationship.

Both Jordan and I have previously come from Marriages with ex partners who either did not know how to be really close who simply refused to.

We are thankful that we don't have that problem with our relationship. In saying that this is something I never want to take for granted, while ever being grateful for a second chance I still make sure that I take the time to be close to my wife every day and night.

It does not take much, only a bit of time and effort to hold her hand, or sit and talk. This is one of many practical examples that helps create that bond of closeness between us both.

Whatever your background, conditioned mindset or past bad experience, having closeness between yourself and another can, if you let it be a wonderful blessing.

Jordan says:

Closeness can mean different things. Ranging from making love to sitting together in warm conversation, each couple has their own.

For example, our close time consists of spending quality time doing such things as retail therapy, going to a movie, having lunch at the local lake, or just watching a movie at home while sitting together holding hands.

Then of course there is the lights out time. Closeness can be seen by those special moments when we show each other how we feel by such things as caressing, kissing gently touching and cuddling each other.

There is no doubt that we all have our own special ways of telling and showing our loved ones how we feel. Remember this, if you don't tell someone close to you how you feel, how will they know?

There is no point in thinking your partner knows this already. From my past experience, I was never told. It did not help my previous relationship but now I am thankful it's a different kettle of fish.

To get told every day that I am loved means so much because it helps maintain that closeness between us. What is being together all about? To me it is be two and one at the same time.

To remain as individuals, to grow into the best we can be, and yet blending our beings through an intimate acquaintance with each other.

The number one ingredient to this unique formula always has been, and always will be-love. They are your world, your every-thing. Everything you do, you do it for that person, and for yourself.

16: WHAT IS PASSION?

Harrison says:
To me, passion is the intense way someone expresses themselves in an intense emotional physical and spiritually strong way. It is in essence holding nothing back from the one you love in your affections.

The act of passion is revealed in a real, total and unpretentious way toward the person you deeply love and care for.

Jordan says:
You know when you feel passionate about something, whether it is cooking, or the love of flowers or your job. Well, I guess feeling passionate about your partner in a relationship is no different, it's just more special.

Passion is something you either have or you don't and the meaning of passion is unique to everyone. Not everyone is the same. Passion, to me is like a spark that ignites inside of me every time I look into Harrison's eyes.

When he is close to me, looking into my eyes it's a real' turn on. The look he gives is so sensual it sets something off and then the passion flows.

17: FEELINGS

Harrison says:
I believe that while feelings are important as part of who we are to express our emotional selves, they should not necessarily be totally relied upon to make decisions or as a gauge to whether you have love or not.

True love is not always based on a feeling but a choice which begins with our thoughts and intent, regardless of how we feel at the time.

You see, feelings can deceive us if they are not at first a continuation of right thoughts, not negative dark ones such as anger, suspicion, bitterness or even jealousy.

Jordan says:
When someone treats you in a manner that is not appropriate, then it has an effect on how you think and feel. Depending on the situation and the type of treatment going through this can leave you feeling low about yourself.

Have you found yourself in a relationship where you are not sure if it's right for you? There could be many reasons why you may not feel comfortable with the person you are with which may cause you to question it.

I found myself in a 23 year relationship where I had mixed feelings at the beginning, at the middle and the end of it. At the beginning I felt like a teenage girl and someone was taking notice of me, giving me time and attention.

In relationships there are a lot of feelings that surface. Sometimes I find myself, just out of the blue looking at my husband, Harrison and falling more in love with him for no reason, then my heart smiles.

In my previous relationship I was hurt. When someone hurts you, you feel down, used, unloved, plus a lot more different feelings depending on your situation and the circumstances.

I know that sometimes it is hard to let go, I have been there myself, but once you choose to your feelings will greatly improve after time.

From experience, you may never forget, that is true, but try and forgive. Doing this not only helps you, but also the people around you for others pick up your mood and it's not fair for your bad, sad dark emotions to be felt by others.

So, although it may take some effort, especially if you have been hurt, try to be positive, work things out and move on, life is too short to do otherwise.

It does make it hard when some people spread lies about you to make themselves look good and to shift the blame, turning others against you. Sadly I am finding this happens very often.

People take sides, especially in families and that makes it hard for new relationships to have a fair go and involve siblings etc. It makes it hard on step relationships and families to have a fair go and a new start.

Some work out and some don't. In any relationship you need to try and keep your feelings on the positive side because negativity can start a whole different ball game.

From my own personal experience I still have times when I feel down, sad and used when it involves a situation concerning my ex-husband and his family.

It is definitely not healthy for yourself or your relationship. Thankfully I have an understanding husband in Harrison who is aware and sees my situation and knows why it makes me feel that way. I hope one day it changes.

18: WHAT IS INTIMACY?

Harrison says:
This important question should never be overlooked when we are considering the wonderful experience of having true love in the life. Intimacy, like so many words in the English language has at times been misinterpreted to mean something it is not.

For instance one perception of intimacy that it refers to a couple of individuals being physically close only that is, either kissing or performing the sexual act. I believe what is overlooked in contrast to this media, Hollywood/,entertainment based mindset is a better and more appropriate meaning to this word.

Intimacy involves a sharing of our true selves from its deepest core, not only our physical selves but our emotional, mental and even to a point our spiritual selves.

This is of course a result of firstly accepting who we are and then fully accepting our partner, giving our total all to each other without fear and falseness.

I believe that there will always be a challenge to anyone no matter who they are, to be able to embrace fully the intimacy that each person is designed to have.

Yet how great and rewarding it is when you become one with another human being. How low we have become when we have before us right now so many opportunities for change, betterment and fuller expression.

So now, while there is opportunity it is time to realize our potential and see that there is nothing wrong with intimacy. Why must we just be as a group of spectators watching life pass us never but really living, simply dragging ourselves around with poor health and poor relationships?

Do you really want to live this way or, grasp to be healthy, to be happy and to know love and experience intimacy in a deep and meaningful way?

In order to do this it may be necessary we must shake off the shackles that many family traditions, societies conditionings, and other false ideas have bound us with. Intimacy is okay. It is not sissy, nor is it wrong, for it is true love expressed in action.

Jordan says:

That is a good question. What is intimacy to you? Do you have it? Why is it important to you? What are you going to do about getting it? I never had it in my previous 23 year relationship, but I know I have it now.

When you go from wanting something, not having it to now I have it all the time, it is very eye opening and satisfying. For me, intimacy can be anything from a loving touch on my shoulder or my side, to a hug, a kiss or a conversation.

Intimacy is where I am being listened to, it is by the eye to eye contact that happens when we have a swing time, sitting on the front porch eating an orange together or just sitting there looking into each other's eyes.

Some people do not like to show affection so does that make them not intimate? I guess in their own way they show it in private.

> 'It is not good enough to live together but remain emotionally distant. Loneliness should be absent. Love builds bridges between lonely hearts to make you close companions for life."

The Love Dare- Day by Day.

Stephen and Alex Kendrick.

19: THREATS TO A RELATIONSHIP

Harrison says:
I am sure you have experienced it or seen it in other's lives. Couples that seem to just exist in their relationship with each other. They barely tolerating each other's company, finding every possible excuse to avoid having that quality time together, the very thing that would revive the flame of emotional love.

If we are not careful, careers, hobbies, time with old mates or even endless hours on the internet social sites, can, if they are allowed to, prevent any real intimacy within a relationship, taking place.

One example how a career can affect intimacy within a relationship is being over committed with your work.

No matter if you are an over efficient manager type who feels he or she can't be done without, even taking work calls on days off, or perhaps the conscientious worker who doesn't know when to stop even when not only their relationship but their health is also suffering greatly.

In order for anyone to have a proper view on what matters most, health and relationships should always be at the top of the priority list and not below your job or career.

There needs to be a cut off time when during the course of the day both parties in the relationship say, enough is enough, let's forget about work and have our quality time together.

Don't get me wrong, work is important, for two reasons, to help us develop our faculties and bring money in, but we need to be balanced in this area otherwise problems start.

Another threat to intimacy is when many past or present friends or acquaintances want to steal a lot of our time or energy with conversation topics which though they may be of interest can still take our focus off the people and matters that mean the most to us. So what really are our priorities what is most important to us?

One of the love languages so often neglected in a relationship is that of quality time together. By the way that is not merely being in the same room or watching a T.V programme, it is talking, and listening, maintaining eye contact and truly giving what the term means, quality time.

Speaking of technology, excessive use of devises such as social media and texting on mobile phones has been found to interfere with the brains proper development to be able to emotionally communicate with another person.

Research has shown that it is apparently linked to the over use of one side of the brain more than the other, the verbal, logical over the expressive, emotional. This, in turn forms a superficial way to deal with others thus preventing true intimacy from being experienced.

As you reflect on what you have read, beware the traps that are out preventing a close union between yourselves from taking place. These snares can come in so many different ways, and in very subtle forms.

There are indeed certain lifestyle habits that can interfere with intimacy between couples occurring. I will make it clearer so as not to be misunderstood, the habits I am referring here to physical habits that cause one to be impatient, irritable or just straight out bad tempered having a short fuse.

Is it any wonder then that as a result of impaired mind and body function, many couples find it difficult to be calm and truly loving with each other especially during those times when certain personal pressures are upon them?

It only takes a short time to realize that by implementing some changes that not only does our health improve but also our temperament.

By drinking more water, having more fresh fruit and vegetables, having a daily exercise program and making sure we get sufficient rest and relaxation can reward us with better health.

Not only that but it can also affect our moods in a positive way making us easier to live with. Having seen the benefits, don't you think it's worth the effort?

Jordan says:

If you are truly and passionately in love and want to be with your partner, you will fight for the forever relationship and to be with that special someone who chose you and you chose to be your life long partner till death do you both part.

These days the marriage vows really mean nothing to a lot of individuals which is a real shame. It is like it is treated as a permission slip to go outside the marriage without any consequences.

20: THE NEED FOR EMPATHY AND COMPASSION

Harrison says:
I believe that in order to maintain intimacy and know what it is like to experience the practical aspect of true love is to cultivate empathy and compassion towards your loved one. For those who are not sure what these words means, I will seek to explain them.

Firstly, empathy refers to the ability and sensitivity to be able to feel for and therefore enter into someone else's pain and struggles without judging them unfairly or thinking they are doing something just for attention or falsely seeking pity.

Closely associated with this term is the word compassion, meaning sincerely pitying within the depth of your being someone in their pain and doing all you can to bring relief to them.

I have personally witnessed a lack of both empathy and compassion from individuals who either through their own insensitivity or as a result of others influence have shown very harsh spirits towards persons who really were struggling physically and emotionally.

Like so many long lost character traits that this present world has sought to take from our hearts, it is I believe not only important but vital that empathy and compassion be restored and daily cultivated especially towards those we claim to love.

Jordan says:
Do you think that empathy and compassion are required in a relationship? Without them how do you communicate and understand the feeling of your partner?

The way I see it is if you have empathy and understanding to see and feel how life's challenges affect our partners, then we will have the compassion needed to support, care and love them till death do us part. You are either a caring person, or you are a selfish one. Which one are you?

> **"True compassion means not only feeling another's pain but also being moved to help relieve it"**
>
> *Daniel Goleman*

21: IS MARRIAGE THE SAME NOW AS IT WAS IN THE PAST?

Harrison says:
The institution of marriage, when recognized the way it is supposed to is a wonderful thing that should cater for many aspects of our lives including the social and emotional areas.

Of course that is the ideal, but sadly, many have wandered far from the original design of this sacred institution which was meant to be one of life's greatest gifts.

One of these reasons is that people seemed to have lost the ability to communicate in such a way as to cross over into that deep, intimate and covenant relationship between each other.

Other things, in many cases interfere like working long hours, troublesome and interfering in laws, other interests in and outside the home and finally the fear of being totally committed in sharing one's life with another person.

People who do it young find it more difficult than they thought. They may not have considered all the factors before marrying. Difficulties or disagreements may be glossed over in the romantic glow of early courtship. No-one is telling you to stay in a marriage anymore.

I believe that today, many people seem to give up before they have even begun, which proves that there is a great need to show that love is based not merely on a surface romantic feeling but on an enduring principle that does not give up easy but applies everything possible to its survival.

Sometimes it relies on nothing but a daily decision to keep loving no matter what the cost. When rightly conducted, marriage, or even initially being in a loving relationship with that someone special is intended to be a wonderful blessing, unfortunately though for many it has become a dreadful curse.

Although admittedly, there may be the odd exception, we as a race of human beings have in many ways wondered very far from the original plan.

Jordan says:

No, I don't think it is. I look back at my parents and grandparents observing that it is so different today.

Most couples from that era stay together and still are. There have been instances where couples have recently celebrated 75 years of marriage, or more which is quite a wonderful achievement.

A lot of people now do not believe in marriage, they prefer to try before they buy and just live together and that's usually where they end up.

When I got married in my previous relationship I believed it was till death do us part because that was how I was brought up, and what I believed to be true. Marriage is a very special commitment that is forever is how I feel about Marriage. Then my parent got divorced and it rocked my world.

Marriage these days is something that is not taken very seriously which is a shame because when you give your whole heart to someone who you love and loves you in return and together your love makes a family, there is no feeling like it in the world.

> **Many marriages would be better if the husband and the wife clearly understood that they are on the same side.**
>
> *Zig Ziglar.*

22: WHY ARE MARRIAGES ENDING AROUND THE 20 to 25 YEAR MARK?

Harrison says:

I once overheard a conversation between two women, one aged between 50-55 who said, I don't even kiss my husband anymore and we have been married 25 years.

She said this as if the reason there was no longer any affection between her and her spouse was because of the length of their married time, as if it had been a jail sentence.

You know one could have a bit of a laugh at the attitude of this woman, but the sad fact is she is not alone, but one among many. Not only are there are there loveless relationships within our society but something else that is noticeably apparent.

It seems to be happening everywhere, decide to call it quits after around the 25 year mark of their marriages. For some, their excuse is that their children are grown up so they are no longer dependent on them because they are now independent young adults.

For others it is claimed that they simply got tired of each other and the spark that was once between them has long died out, or the grass is greener on the other side, meaning someone better coming along not being happy with their first choice, or wanting a younger version.

Perhaps the mid-life crisis that some, particularly men seem to go through prompts then to look for a younger woman to help him regain his youthful passion and to lift his ego with the thought that at least one female finds him still attractive.

It could be the secretary or another one of his work mates that he has become infatuated with because of her friendly smile that greets him when they are on the job together.

Or perhaps the sneaky way he has looked up those dating, matchmaking internet sites behind his wife's back, then telling her how he is going to a business meeting when the only meeting he has planned is a sexual one with his mistress.

Many women fall into the same trap, although from what I understand it's more because of the emotional need instead of the physical. Of course there may be exceptions to the rule.

Whatever the reason or excuse is, is breaking up really the solution if there is no foul play or abuse? Could there possibly be a way for couples to start afresh their lives, to recommit to each other.

For this to happen, the reality is that many couples may have to build on a foundation that involves a totally new way of thinking that involves putting into practice the concepts covered in this book.

Loneliness even within a marriage can take place. We all have emotional love tanks that require filling, whether it be by quality time, acts of service, gifts, words of affirmation, or physical touch.

So whatever primary love language you or your spouse have if they are neglected, the love tank remains empty. What these all mean in detail are outlined in the described in the book, 'The five love languages' by Gary Chapman .1991'

Here is a quote from this very interesting and enlightening book. Once you identify and learn to speak you spouse's primary love language, I believe that you will have discovered the key to a long lasting, loving marriage'.

Love need not evaporate after the wedding, but in order to keep it alive most of us will have to put forth the effort to learn a secondary love language. We cannot rely on our native tongue if our spouse does not understand it.

If we want him or her to feel the love we are trying to communicate, we must express it in his or her primary love language." The five love languages. Gary Chapman .1991

No matter what age any one is, young or old, the facts are still the same, if we allow love to grow cold it will. If no effort is made to keep alive that spark it will die out.

If a couple has begun to neglect each other, years ago it will not improve until a mutual decision is make to do whatever it takes to regain that lost love?

Jordan says:
I am noticing more than ever, how many relationships are ending around the 20 to 25 year mark. I was one of these statistics. Why is this? I guess from the conversations we hear, or see in our friend's relationships, or their friend's situations, it seems to be the same sort of reasons.

You can be in a relationship and not know at the time things are not right, but then after it's all over you put it all together and realize the signs were there but we just didn't see them, or we did, but chose to ignore them, because we were just in the comfortable zone as we had been for all those years.

When you first get together it's all new and exciting and sexual and lustful, then it moves to the engagement, the wedding then the children and buying the family home.

You then get into a routine and become comfortable. It gets to be a get up go to work come home have a meal go to bed and start again. When all this is going on where is the together time?

This is why affairs, and work friendships happen because there's a lot of hours at work with colleagues of the opposite sex, or boredom because one partner is always at work or somewhere else, as the internet is another option.

Someone once referred to being married for 25 years as a prison sentence now I am on parole and free to look again, or the grass is a lot greener on the other side. These are the answers to why they have ended the relationship, which is no real answer at all.

Marriage has always been a freedom of choice for each individual, so if necessary, it's their choice to end it but there is a right way and a wrong way to do it, and most people choose the wrong way even though hurting the other person is never a thought or a care to them.

A lot of people only think about themselves and where the blame lays when other people find out, not that it is anyone else's business.

Some people can't handle the truth getting out and tend to blame the other person for what they did in order to keep themselves in the good books of everyone. That is so wrong in so many ways, as it effects not only the people in the relationship but the whole family, and it is very selfish.

Then there's the after effects. The children and what effect all this has on them. The taking of sides because of lies and family loyalty even when lies are involved, causing a rift and split in the family.

Sometimes the wrong person comes out smelling like roses while the innocent partner is blamed, shunned and treated badly having children call that person names, being disrespectful, and being abusive to the parent who loved them and gave up so many years of their life for them.

The splitting of a family is always a traumatic experience for everyone concerned and in very few cases do the ex-partners get along for the sake of the children.

It is usually the selfish and the one to save face who makes things complicated, and keeps the family apart for the power. Some people get off on hurting others as well making the situation wrong again.

Some other excuses I have heard of is I didn't have a social life, or my wife was sick all the time. What happened to the vows we said for better or worse, in sickness and in health till death do us part?

23: WHY DO PARTNERS STRAY?

Harrison says:
There are many reasons that may lead to partners to stray. The starting point is that something is lacking in their present relationship, namely intimacy, communication or attraction to each other.

Instead of seeking to restore this by having quality time together, getting counselling or fighting to put the spark back into their marriage one of the partners strays. A lonely, discontented heart by either sex can be dawn to venture into forbidden ground.

This can happen in a very subtle way and in various forms such as secretly looking on the online dating sites or getting over familiar with one of their co-workers who are of the opposite sex.

In my opinion many relationships that may have grown cold, or if one partner has become discontented, are in danger of having a third party come between them if they are not careful.

Jordan says:
A lot of couples who have young or even teenage families stay together for the kid's sake. But when you think about it, how is being in a home seeing two unhappy parents helping their children?

They say that the grass is always greener on the other side- but is it really? It just causes more misery and pain then sadly the children usually get caught up in the middle. What happens when you go to the 'greener side'? Why do you stray?

Whether it's a male or female it's all the same. Usually it's because one or both are not happy in their current relationship. But by having an affair doesn't help or fix the problem in the first place.

Why don't couples talk about their problems? Whether it be to each other, to a counselor, at least it's a start. Some partners tell themselves they are not happy and things will be better with someone new, but really what does that do?

It breaks up a family, causes stress, traumatizes the children, and in most cases causes a very uncomfortable environment and relationship afterwards, and why?

All because one partner thinks they can do better than the original choice of a loving partner they made all those years ago. Some people are not willing to work for something they should treasure.

> **If you want to keep from becoming infatuated - hands off and three feet distance - must be the rule. The bigger part of yielding to temptation is proximity.**
>
> **The nearer you get to temptation, the more sure you are of falling into it and yielding to it.**

The farther we keep away from temptation, the safer we are. Greater distance means greater assurance of staying victorious. Some people wonder why they are always falling into temptation.

The answer is simple. They got too close to it. Infatuation is just that way. The closer you get to someone you shouldn't be near, the more possible it is for you to become infatuated.

Then ABCs of Bible prayer.

Coon, Paster Glenn.

24: WHAT IS HURTFUL TO YOU IN YOUR RELATIONSHIP?

Harrison says:
This is a good question and can have many different answers depending on everyone's unique circumstance. From my past experience, before I met Jordan the thing that was the most hurtful for me was that my opinion was not respected nor my role as both a husband and then as a father.

I'm sure there have been many men who have had this happen to them, some maybe have deserved this some have not. Either way for whatever reason this has occurred it can be very hurtful and undermining especially when a man's opinion and, or role has been replaced by another as was my case. That is now in my past, and much of the pain from those days is long gone and healed thanks a lot to having Jordan in my life.

Jordan says:
Being with your partner for whatever period of time and not ever hearing I love you from them, or hearing I don't love you anymore?'

Which of these hurts your heart and makes you cry? Do you want to be told I love you? Some people do and some don't. Men think that women don't need to hear it from them.

Well, I'm here to tell you that both men and women, deep down need to hear it or at least be shown it one way or another.

I did not have that in my first marriage, but I did fall in and out of love with my ex-husband even though he did cheat on me for nearly all of our relationship.

I don't really know what kind of love it was, thinking about it now that I know and have what I feel in my heart true love is.

25: CAN TRUE LOVE EXIST IF ONE PARTNER WANTS TO CONTROL OR DEGRADE THE OTHER?

Harrison says:

A relationship either as a marriage or otherwise may have, on face value some form of stability, even last for years but with close examination it is seen to have no real substance to it.

You see, as has been discussed already true love is demonstrated in the unselfish sharing of two lives each seeking the betterment of the other.

Two deadly elements that destroy this from taking place is when one partner wants to control the other or degrade them. I will begin with the subject of control.

This can be shown in many ways such as not letting them make a decision for themselves, making them do something that they feel uncomfortable about or basically robbing the partner of any free independent choices.

For instance doing the things they like including who to enjoy quality time with, and even how to spend their money.

It is obvious that someone would naturally feel degraded when they are being controlled constantly that is true, combined with that is either name calling of simply being treated like an inferior, even as an adult might relate to a child.

This is probably the worst thing that anyone could do to someone. It borders on the fringes of abuse. For anything done that has the potential to damage someone's self-worth and dignity, whether it be physical, emotional or financial does just that abuse!

Of course excuses are often made by these deceived control freaks like, he or she could not make their minds up so I did it for them, or they were treated like they deserved.

In some cases this may be true but, still there is no cause to control or degrade the partner you claim to love, the person you may have spent many years with. The person who at one time in their life chose to unite with you thinking that it would not only take away their loneliness but help them feel loved and valued as an equal, not an inferior.

Jordan says:

To me a relationship is a two way street where each partner brings strengths and weaknesses and they complement each other. One does not overtake the other.

Both partners should be supporting and loving to each other no matter what because that is what marriage is about.

Decisions should be made together, as a team, and yes there will always be a positive and negative side to everything, but don't let the sun go down with bad blood between you.

In some relationships the green monster does rear its ugly head and that does cause issues and jealousy between partners.

Then abuse can set in, which then makes the controlling partner feel more in control. The situation can then escalate and life and the relationship can become toxic.

If there are any children in the relationship it becomes dangerous, as the children are used as pawns between the partners, and the controlling partner can then use the children to manipulate the other partner. This is a very sad situation and another family is split up.

I have also noticed that a lot of women's body change after child birth because of hormonal issues, causing some partners to degrade them because they are not slim and their breasts pointing to the sky like they used to be when they first met. This is a very shallow attitude to have.

Hello, all bodies change both men and women's in the different stages of their lives and for various reasons.

To be told you are big, fat and ugly every day for so many years all because you had your partner's children is not a reason to be degraded.

Child birth and being a mother is a very honorable career to have because some women are not able to have children, yet they too are degraded in some way for other reasons. Both being controlled and degraded is so wrong on any level and it is a selfish narcistic person who does it.

> **"Neither the husband nor the wife should attempt to exercise over the other arbitrary control.**
>
> **Do not compel each other to yield to your wishes.**

You cannot do this and retain each other's love.

Be kind, patient and forbearing, considerate and courteous.

By the grace of God you can succeed in making each other happy as in the marriage vow you promised to do."

The Ministry of Healing p 361

– E.G. White.

26: WHY DO SOME WOMEN SEEM TO ATTRACT SELFISH AND ABUSIVE MEN?

Harrison says:
I have seen this happen again and again. Maybe you have to? Perhaps you may be one of those women?

Either way, this has perplexed me, especially when I believe that the women in question here could do so much better. Now I am not talking about their looks merely but who they are as people, their personalities, goals and values. One explanation is the low opinion they have on themselves.

In many cases this mindset goes right back to when they were children or an adolescent, when they had an estranged relationship with their fathers. Perhaps they either were abused or had a sense of rejection.

The result is for the years following they try and find that missing ingredient in their lives of having a male take notice of them, to give them affection, to simply give them time and attention.

Unfortunately there are many selfish men who have taken advantage on these lonely hearted, hurting women. These Prince Charming types do more harm than good.

They initially present themselves as someone they can trust, then having allured these women on step by step they show their true colors as abusers.

Many of these men are immature little boys who may have their own issues of identity and insecurity they are dealing with, and so have no idea how to love someone in an understanding, warm and unselfish way that would bring healing to their wives or partners.

Then, there is the problem that many women face, finally accepting the sad fact that for their good, it is time to break from this relationship.

Year after year they may have endured the pain, the abuse, and the humiliation of themselves hoping that things will one day improve or perhaps excusing the narcissistic behavior of their partner.

In spite of that thought, because in many cases things don't get better, and the woman's confidence is shattered, their self -worth has diminished greatly and in the midst of their emotional turmoil they may even feel a sense of false guilt when the thought of leaving crosses their mind.

Some perhaps may want to leave but are fearful of doing so because of the risk of having their ex-partner coming after them, to do them harm in some way in spite of that though some summon up the courage to do so anyway regardless of the consequences.

Jordan says:
We all look at the opposite sex and we are either attracted to them or not for whatever reason. Sometimes what we are attracted to on the outside is not the same as on the inside.

Have you heard the expression beautiful, beautiful. This means that a person is beautiful on the outside and on the inside. To me Harrison is this, as he says I am to him.

Then there are ugly ugly. This means that that person is ugly on the inside and the outside. You can also have an ugly beautiful where the person is one on the outside and the other on the inside and visa versa.

Some women attract all the ones that are not beautiful beautiful and find they are being used or abused or both.

They seem to attract this type because they have a very low self- esteem, no confidence or desperate to be loved they go with whoever comes along and shows them attention accepting whatever treatment comes with it.

This is wrong on so many levels because of something that may have happened in their past life, whether it be no father in their lives, not a good relationship with their father, or from being abused.

Why should a women stand for that? Every human being is given free choice and what they do with that shapes their futures and their lives, and only they can change that.

If this is you please reach out for help, as you are special and deserve a happy fulfilling life of joy, laughter and love.

27: STANDING TALL AND MOVING FORWARD

Harrison says:
If untruths have been spread about you, although it can be testing and admittedly hurtful it is important to recognize them for what they are, just lies and untruths. Abuse, trauma, negativity, darkness and pain can take a long time to be fully healed from, even years.

It is with time, true friendships and an acceptance of your uniqueness that enables this process to take place in a proactive way. It is hard at times to stand tall and move forward particularly if your previous relationship left you emotionally drained and feeling unloved, and unworthy of anyone's care and affections.

Indeed the dark spiritual element that inspired your ex-partner to say and do those terrible things will continue to try and keep you down by his cruel whispering suggestions.

Again it is important to recognize these thoughts as lies and untruths. A greater power will inspire and strengthen you to never give up, to realize not only your worth but also your potential.

You will be amazed at how things will begin happening for you, people, books DVDs and any other helpful resource will come into your life. You have chosen to take that step forward and you are not alone.

From my understanding, we have been designed to love deeply and fully. What we see around us in messed up relationships is simply the results of an enemy that has sought to destroy something that could be beautiful if the right principles combined with the right power were put in it.

Selfishness comes in its various forms such as addictions, unfaithfulness, greed, and, simply jumbled priorities wrecks relationships.

Don't wait to first be involved in an abusive relationship to see that there is room for improvement. If you both willing to slowly and steadily make whatever changes then what a difference you will notice.

But be aware it is a daily walk effort that is needed. It is the little things done and said every day that will make up the sum total of the way a loving relationship can be.

Jordan says:

Sometimes it is very hard after a relationship breakdown to move forward, remembering everyone's circumstance are different.

Everyone is a special individual who deserves to be happy in their lifetime, whether their choice is in a relationship or single till you find the right partner.

Moving forward is sometimes not as easy as you may think it is. People can put on a great front and smile and pretend to be happy to please others when really inside their heart is breaking and they are hurt and devastated.

These people wait till they are alone to show their grief and suffer in silence. This can go on for years.

When there is a rift between a parent and their children it does go on for years, which is very wrong, sad and quite unnecessary.

A parent loves their child unconditionally no matter how they treat them, and the child should show always their parent respect no matter what.

Trying to move on can sometimes be very hard to do especially when you have negativity against you from your ex-partner, his family, and his new partner influencing the children.

You are always told to let it go and move on. That is alright for everyone to say but if you are a person that takes everything to heart then you find it hard, especially when your ex-partner is supposed to be on a friendly basis with you because children are involved, then the new partner moves in and that all changes, and then because of insecurities you are shunned and pushed aside, only to be replaced and forgotten.

How could you move on in a situation like this? Very slowly, very heartbroken and very sad. Time is supposed to heal all wounds. I think it can when positive things start to happen to you.

You can only go day by day and deal with what confronts you as it comes.

> **Stand Tall, Stand Proud. Know that you are unique and magnificent. You do not need the approval of others.**
>
> *Jonathan Lockwood Huie*

28: INTERNET RELATIONSHIPS

Harrison says:
Internet relationships via the social media and some dating sites seem very appealing to young and old alike. While it is true there perhaps has been a lot of success stories as a result of using this means to meet someone special, there also can be an element of risk.

To those looking for love or even a friend on the internet be very cautious, there are a lot of desperate predators out there who are looking for a victim to use, abuse or perhaps worse.

In this world we have become so used to relying on our computers for so many things, even socializing, and because of that a lot of people, particularly the young tend to be very naïve about what they say on the internet and who they communicate with.

Be careful about what you say about yourself and be cautious when Mr or Mrs Charmer makes contact with you and who promise the world. It is best to question their intentions if they seem to be coming on too strong too quickly.

If on the other hand after getting to know someone for a while you feel comfortable about what is developing between you and a mutual decision is made to meet, it is best for a while to make sure it is in a public place like a café and definitely during the day-night time meetings with someone can pose a risk especially to women who may be not awake to the potential dangers.

Am I making you paranoid? I hope not but at the same time it doesn't pay to be too careless either.

Jordan says:
I find the internet a fascinating, complicated, helpful tool but can be very dangerous and a bad distraction when there are problems in a relationship.

If you are a single person looking that's fine. Hands and minds can wonder very easily, when there is any sign of trouble in paradise.

Either partner, could meet someone on line, and that can make them feel special because someone new is taking an interest in them, as their partner has not done that in years, whether it's because of children taking up all their time, or work commitments or they are just tired and rundown.

You can lust after someone else, you don't have to sleep with them, but this is still adultery because you are looking outside of the relationship.

Then when you meet someone on line there is the secrecy of messages and phone calls and secret meetings and then there is the pictures that are being sent.

Once you start all this there is no going back. Then there is when your partner finds out. Then the consequences flow, which completely slipped your mind when you started all this.

All of this is wrong when you have a loving partner and are in a committed relationship.

If you are unhappy sit down and talk to your partner and explain the problem, try and work it out before something beautiful ends nastily.

29: WHY ARE WE TOGETHER?

Harrison says:
Have you ever asked yourself or your partner this question? It is often a good starting point for change when it comes as a harsh reality that perhaps you and the person you are with might be together for the wrong reason.

While walking through one of the shopping centres some time back, we ran into someone we hadn't seen for a while who broke the news to us that he and his wife had recently split up.

After getting over the initial shock, the question was asked what had happened, the man's answer was simple we lost our business, there was no money coming in so she said it was best they separated.

To us and to this man this was a very shallow excuse, maybe there were other issues we don't know but the fact is there's is not an isolated case that is why we have titled this section Why are we together?

Was there a time when love bound your hearts and you swore that you you'd be ever there for each other, maybe at the marriage alter itself you spoke those well-known vows, in sickness and in health, for richer and poorer for better or worse as long as we both shall live.

But when the test comes, many lives unfortunately show how shaky their foundation is and their house comes crumbling down. Look, we understand that there are pressures on couples and families everywhere but why should we allow that fact to pull us apart.

From my own personal perspective things like the example of what I referred to should never happen because Jordan and myself have been in that situation and we are still together so either the love and commitment for each other is strong and real or it is not.

We have gone through tough times together, but it has brought us closer together not pulled us apart like it does some.

Jordan says:

This is a very honest question which should have a very honest answer. Why are you? Is it because your relationship is one of convenience? Maybe it's just comfortable because it has been so many years it's like a routine.

Are you staying together for your children? If so do you think this is fair to them and to both of you? We all have to live with our choices and I hope if one of the above is you that it is a choice you are happy to live with.

I know that Harrison and I are together because we truly love each other with all our hearts. I know I can trust him and never have to worry about him straying or even looking at another women because he believes in Marriage and what it stands for.

> **Love is fundamental to the success of your marriage.**
>
> **Not your current feelings of romance or sexual satisfaction.**

Not a stronger financial standing or even your spouse's behavior.

All these can circumstantially change, and they will.

But when storms rise and conditions worsen, love driven marriages endure and work through even the toughest issues without giving up."

The Love Dare- Day by Day.

Stephen Kendrick and Alex Kendrick.

30: WHAT KEEPS US TOGETHER / WHAT TEARS US APART?

Harrison says:

It is an important couple of questions to ask ourselves. What does keep us together and what tears us apart? The first thing to ask is what was the reason we got together in the first place?

Is it because we did not want to be alone. Did you want someone to have a business partnership with or simply because there was genuine attraction between 2 people and it resulted in a loving relationship.

So, what keeps us together? Is it our work, our interests, our hobbies or simply our children? By contrast, what tears us apart?

Is it our bad habits, harsh words, how we spend our time or putting other things before our relationship such as our work, friends or preferring to spent time in front of the T.V instead of sitting quietly with our partner talking about those things that really matter like how to enhance our emotional love in the home.

These questions are something we all need to ask ourselves if we feel that there is a problem in our marriages or even newly established relationships.

Jordan says:

What keeps us together? Our love for each other does. Also the similarities we have, the interests we share and our kind caring hearts for other human beings.

We are very loving and caring people who fit together like a glove. We even end each other's sentences, and if I said to Harrison can I please ask you to do something for me, he would know what I was going to say even before I said it, that is how much in sync we are together.

We will be celebrating our 10 year anniversary soon with a renewal of our vows to each other, in front of all the important people in our lives.

What tears us apart? This can be answered from a lot of other people's experiences. We can talk about the usual ones like cheating, straying, leaving, affairs, betrayal, and the list goes on.

Once it all becomes known it causes a whirlwind and once the trust has been lost there's usually no going back.

Those of you who have been there know what I am talking about. The sadness from all this is if there is children involved, the innocent parties.

31: THE NEED FOR AFFECTION

Harrison says:
From my experience, love cannot flourish without giving and receiving affection. On this subject, I will reveal something you may find quite interesting and even perhaps inspiring.

Recently I told Jordan why I like to kiss her. There are at least 5 reasons. They are it is a way to show my love to her. It is a natural thing for me to do to be close to her. It feels good. It tastes good, and it helps me maintain my love tank as physical touch is one of my love languages.

Of course there are other forms of affection that we display between ourselves such as walking hand in hand, holding each other close and I will leave what else to your imagination, for I think you know what I am leading to.

Affection is vital to a relationship, as I read in a book recently, couples need to keep in touch with each other in order to maintain that special intimacy.

I am not too sure whether you realize it or not but we have tiny very sensitive nerve endings called tactile receptors beneath our skin surface that thrives on touch. These in turn send a message to our brains that gives us a sense of comfort, love and security as the feeling of emotional nurturing sweeps over us.

Can anyone relate to this experience, who has ever had a relaxing or a sensual massage? Even something simple like a touch on your shoulder or the back of your hand can have the same effect and it can only bring two people close and not alienate them from each other.

You see, there perhaps never has been such a vital time in earth's history to really get close to you loved one for in many homes and relationships there is a gross indifference everywhere to do so.

Jordan says:

As humans we love and need touch. It sends special sensations to us in all sorts of places depending on the circumstances. As mothers when we have a baby we bond with him or her through touch.

Affection to me is many things, one being touch, whether it is giving someone a backrub or a massage. Cuddling, holding, caressing, holding hands, hugging or kissing. All of the gestures are a sign of affection to the person you love.

It can also be making the time to spend with your partner, anticipating their needs. Do you know your partner's love language?

Do you give your partner your full attention? Do you completely listen to them while making eye contact?

Your partner needs to know you love and care for them and the need for affection is part of a relationship.

Remember your partner needs you to touch them and show affection as it is a way of showing you love them.

32: WHAT ARE SIGNS OF AFFECTION?

Harrison says:
This of course is up to the individual, but for me, it's about doing things together like holding hands, kissing, or giving a full body massage.

Not forgetting, of course the wonderful experience of gazing into each other's eyes, feeling cared and secure in one another's presence. It's about simply saying with sincerity and meaning I love you.

All of us, in our own, unique way that is, according to our personalities and love languages will show what signs of affection works for us in our relationship with each other best.

I now address you men. It is a good thing to show affection, most women are craving more, not just a lustful, very casual and empty relationship that has only the trimmings of what it should be, or as it has become so often, a business partnership. Some perceive acting macho is what being a real "man" is all about.

To you women, who have perhaps gone to the other extreme, if your man wants to really show you love, do you let him? Don't allow the false ideals and corrupt fake role models everywhere try to shape you into something you are not.

To be your true self amidst a lot of fake standards and people takes moral courage and certain individuals may not like you because you dare to be genuine, but who cares, at least you are happy who you are and that's all that matters.

The question that exists in many minds is, what is the very best way to do the things outlined in this book? Like every major change that we make in life, it all starts with a decision, a willing choice to let go of the old and grasp the new way, which we believe is the 'best' way.

Jordan says:

The thought of someone being affectionate with me scared me a little considering where I had come from. In my previous relationship the affection I was used to was a big zero, nothing.

The affection I dreamed of and wanted was what I saw on the television in the movies. I know it's only made up but to me when I was watching it, it seemed so real, but that was what I wanted.

To be touched softly, but in a loving way. To be cuddled like someone really loved me. To be looked at like there was nobody else, just me.

There are all different ways to show affection. A loving touch on a shoulder, or a waste, a gentle kiss on the forehead or the cheek, even a holding of a hand.

My favorite sign of affection with Harrison is when we sit and watch a romantic movie together holding hands, then he comes and kneels in front of me and kisses me passionately.

He looks into my eyes and tells me he loves me, smiles, then touches my face lovingly. He also makes me a special sandwich sometimes and puts a loving note with it on the serviette. I have kept them all and put them in our picture frames to keep forever.

Affection I think is an important part of a relationship because when time gets away as it does sometimes, and the pressures of daily routines, it doesn't leave a lot of time for affection, so the tiniest little gesture will mean a lot.

So what is your gesture of affection? What is your love language?

33: TIME

Harrison says:
I have noticed that life in society over the last couple of decades has particularly got more and more hurried and intense. The financial strain on many individuals and families causes them to feel that they must sacrifice time for their health and for each other in order to make a living.

A great number wake early in the morning, maybe having a breakfast of coffee and toast then perhaps spending a short time with their partners and or children before driving on the busy freeway or travelling on a crowded train to their workplace.

Then at the end of a tiring day the grim task of facing the homebound commuting is experienced until they stagger through the front door at home with barely enough time or energy for that person or people that should matter most.

I have been on that course of action so I know how tiring it can be. Not only that, but I have experienced first how this can effect a relationship. A few years back though I decided to re-prioritize and make better use of my time.

I now make sure I have time for 3 things even before I do any work. They are time for quiet prayer and reflection every day, time for my health, particularly focusing on nutritional diet and adequate rest, and time for the enhancement of my marriage.

Then, having made these things priority I can look for ways to bring in money whether by working away or from home whatever suits my skills and current circumstance.

Some people who read this may think it is either lazy or impractical in this faced paced world-but is it really? Perhaps we need to reassess what really matters.

Is there possibly a need to reflect on why there are some many sick and tired individuals barely getting by in their lives and relationships? Maybe it is high time to stop and reflect on how to make better use of time.

Jordan says:

As I watch people, I notice a 'hurried' pace within them. They hurry to catch transport, get to their work, eat their meals, smoke their cigarettes and sip coffee on their breaks.

All this is because to 'hurry' is the way of the world especially in the city lifestyle. Their relationships no doubt run at the same pace-hurried. Do they ever consider to slow things down a little?

It's not as though it would hurt them. It's a wonder that with all this hurrying and rushing that every single person doing this isn't as thin as a stick. No real time for anything worthwhile in their life.

The life I mean is to put that necessary time into love and relationships, but sadly most people seem to live by the clock. If people put the time required into all aspects of their lives that really matter, I'm sure it would run a lot smoother.

There would be less stress, less sickness and definitely less marriage or family breakdowns. What time do you give to your family, your kids, your partner and yourself?

What time do you have to relax? When was the last time you had a manicure or a pedicure or even a night out with the girls or boys? How long has it been since you went out for dinner or to the movies as a couple? So what are you going to do about it?

34: TIME TOGETHER

Harrison says:
In this crazy and sometimes overly fast past world I have found it takes a decided daily choice and effort to make sure that we have that special quiet time together.

Many things can distract us for doing this if we are not careful as I'm sure you are aware even being busy anf activities can take up so much of our time and energies that we sometimes need to put the brakes on to sit quietly together, to take a breath and reconnect.

Romance is one aspects of true love that can ever remain strong. The way that this can happen may differ from one couple to another but nevertheless I believe it is essential to a well-balanced intimate relationship.

A warm kiss, a loving embrace and a quiet moment sharing words that belong only to each other all of these things and even many more all add up to help enhance the love that Jordan and I have.

If you reader long for a real closeness with your partner then, my advice is to make quiet times together part of your priority.

Jordan says:
Time is a precious commodity. Most people spend 8-10 hours asleep, 8-10 hours at work nearly every day then by the time you shower, relax, and it's bedtime again.

I personally love the, you and me time. We do a thing called swing time. This can be a few different things. It can be sitting on the step eating oranges and talking like Harrison and I do.

It can be lying together on the bed talking or cuddled up watching T.V. Sometimes we just sit there and look at each other smiling and not saying a word.

My personal favorite is lying on our king size bed, head to toe while Harrison does reflexology on my feet. We talk, we laugh, spend quality time together.

Spending quality time together does not mean you have to always go out, such as a movie, dancing, or socializing.

The partner you choose to be in a relationship with is your choice, and you need to find your own way to spend time with each other, to whatever suits your relationship and circumstance.

What are special times? Special times are the time to do things together. It doesn't matter it is cuddling on the couch, talking on bed, laughing at the movies or holding hands on a walk.

It's all about doing things together. That means both of you being in the same place together at the same time. Being romantic can mean many things. It can be bringing home flowers, receiving a love letter/card. Being given a poem, or even a box of chocolates.

Romance isn't necessary being given things. It can mean a romantic dinner together, going to the movies, a walk on the beach, holding each other's hands and of course looking into each other's eyes without saying a word.

35: SPENDING TIME TOGETHER WHEN YOU HAVE CHILDREN

Harrison says:

I truly believe that no matter what your situation if you really want to, it is possible to be loving and affectionate within a relationship.

There should be no exceptions to this no, not even because you have children. Husbands and wives can adapt as their situation allows by making sure they still allow their love to stay strong between them.

I believe also that young ones from toddlers to teenagers need to have good role models before them and what better way but by their parents showing them an example of tender true love between each other.

The father can show his son's how to treat a women and the mother can show her daughters how to treat a man.

Jordan says:

One of the objections that we have often encountered from couples with families is that they find it difficult to maintain an intimate relationship with your spouse if you have children.

Is this true, or perhaps for some, simply an excuse? Is it possible to be hot towards each other even when you do have your children in the household with you?

You can do things with your children around. It doesn't take a lot to reach out and just hold your love one. Whether it be a touch on their shoulder or backside as they pass by, or perhaps a wink or a smile.

All it really takes is a daily decision and a bit of an effort on both parties and you will be amazed at what can result.

Concerning the question on being romantic being romantic can mean many things. It can be bringing home flowers, receiving a love letter or a card. Being given a poem, or even a box of chocolates.

Romance isn't necessary being given things. It can mean a romantic dinner together, going to the movies, a walk on the beach, holding each other's hands and of course looking into each other's eyes without saying a word. As I said, all it takes is a decision and a bit of an effort- are you willing to give it a try?

You can do things with children around. It doesn't take a lot to reach out and just touch your loved one. Whether it be a touch on their shoulder / backside as you pass by or a wink with a smile.

To add to this thought I have found this quote which emphasizes the importance of parents showing affection in front of their children.

36: HOW CAN A MAN MAKE A WOMAN FEEL GOOD ABOUT HERSELF?

Harrison says:

From a man's point of view I have realized that to help a woman feel good about herself is to love and accept her unconditionally.

She needs to be treated like a queen, that is with honor and respect in spite of the way she may have felt about herself before you met her.

Many woman such as my precious wife Jordan may have come for a previous relationship with someone who treated them disrespectfully, which causes them to feel low about themselves.

In some cases she may feel unworthy of being truly loved and honored, but with much consistent tender love and care a woman who may have been emotionally bruised can begin to heal.

As a result and with a new bright outlook she will hopefully start to feel good about herself.

Jordan says:

Being a large woman, what makes me feel good is Harrison wanting to love me including all the extra bits of me that are over the normal size I should be, and wish that I was.

Telling me I'm beautiful, loved appreciated and wanted everyday as he does is now starting to get into my head.

As I have explained to him, when you have been told you are big, fat and ugly for 23 years of your life you tend to believe it. When you look in the mirror, no matter what, you see it. That's not going to change overnight.

It has been over 3 years now and I'm feeling comfortable enough to leave the light on at bedtime and to see me in the light. When he does he touches all of me and says he loves all of me every day because it's part of me.

37: OUR RELATIONSHIP

Harrison says:
I appreciate the description that Jordan has given in regards to how the things I do makes her feel like a woman, but you know, it gets down to this fact, the values and principles that I chose to live can only enhance a relationship.

In my opinion, the difference is it's the choice in making God's ways my own, I have some quiet time with Him every day in prayer and ask for the strength to be the best I can be as a loving and faithful husband.

I personally know that to me, it is the best way with a sure and steady foundation that I have tried to build on I believe will eventually fall.

Jordan says:
I personally find myself in a new relationship after being in an old relationship with someone for 23 years. The differences between the two men is so significant.

One is a kind, loving, honest, generous, giving, committed to a relationship man; the other was a nasty, selfish, narcissistic liar who cared only about himself. One is deep, the other is shallow.

These men are like chalk and cheese. One is the opposite; the other is the same as me with a kind, caring and giving heart.

They say opposites attract. Well, I had an opposite for 23 years. He did attract and we were fine for a while but after that it wasn't nice.

What, I'm finding is when you are in a relationship with someone who has the same values, traits, likes etc as you, life runs so smoothly and feels as natural as the wind blowing in your hair or the sun shining in your face.

When a partner is considerate, they have the other person as their priority. I know this because my new partner is very considerate.

He looks at me in many ways, just as I am a considerate partner too always looking out for his best.

Some people wonder if there is a look of love. I say yes. Harrison looks at me with such a looking his eyes it has to be love. His eyes sparkle and it looks like they are smiling at me.

I used to wonder who or what he was looking at, but now I know for sure now he is looking at me. How do I know this?

Well, when there are only two of us in the room I know that for sure. Apart from his body language, facial expression and demeanor, his eyes are like they are mesmerized as he moves towards me and the passionate embrace I feel from his lips and his body shows there's no mistaking, it's definitely ME.

While we were both studying at home doing courses, we found it hard to keep our hands off each other, so we decided on having an agreement otherwise no studying would get done.

The way we got around this was to set an alarm and every 30 minutes we would have a kiss and cuddle break. It worked well.

Oh, by the way, in between that break we would find ourselves touching hands across the table, smiling and winking at one another.

It was amazing how fast the 30 minutes went and yes we actually did get some study done. Our breaks used to be 15 minutes, we had to change them to appreciate them more, and because we weren't getting anything productively done otherwise.

Harrison means so much to me that for our wedding I wrote a song for him that I sang at the wedding reception.

For the words to come to me I sat and thought about everything he does for me and how it makes me feel. I guess you could say then the words came easy.

If you are fortunate enough to be in a relationship where you have married your soul mate, and are truly loved, deeply meaningfully, and whole, then you are the luckiest person in the world.

38: MY VIEW ON MEN

Jordan says:
How do women really feel about men? A question that has been asked I'm sure for many years now, and will still be asked for many, many more. Well, luckily for women there are a lot of different men out there as no woman wants the same thing in a man.

Some things may vary here and there in different categories. Some women want the macho man, some want the man's man, some want a romantic man, some a down to earth man, some a wild man, some an athletic man, some a happy go lucky man, or some a real honest down to earth Godly man with principles like I have.

When my friends see me with Harrison they want someone just like him. The usual line then comes into play. Do you have a brother?

Some women say they want one type of man but then settle with another. I wish that today the men teaching their sons how to treat a woman for their future was all good and positive things with no nastiness, violence, put downs, or abuse in any way shape or form, because it's a case of monkey see, monkey do.

39: MY VIEW ON WOMEN

Harrison says:
Each man I'm sure has his own view on what he sees in women. It depends on what he may have seen growing up, perhaps in the example of his mother or any other females that he saw in his younger years or since then.

How he views women can also have been due to many influences that have shaped his attitude like in the medium of entertainment and media as was mentioned in the chapter 'the shaping of societies thinking. '

I have encountered such false impressions since my youth but now I firmly believe that the only true way a woman is to be viewed and indeed, valued is through the way our Creator has designed them to be.

I know from experience that a woman is a unique counterpart of man. It is therefore my view that a woman can complement a man, that she can be to him and for him emotionally, physically, socially and sexually what someone of the same sex was not designed to be.

I have had male friends over the years and it is good to have some mates to chat with and be pals to but it has been only with a woman, especially with one who is willing to be her true and emotional expressive self that I have felt compete.

> **Men and women have strengths that complement each other.**

Edwin Louis Cole

40: THOUGHTS

Harrison says:
It is truly a beautiful experience to wake up next to someone who really loves and appreciates me, as I do with her. Before I met Jordan I thought I knew what love was all about but I didn't really.

To reach out to and admire with true love my spouse simply because of who she is fills my mind with heartfelt gratitude as a new day begins.

Life is a gift and to share it with someone who is moving in the same direction as me has made it complete. I am indeed eternally grateful for this wonderful opportunity.

Jordan says:
Laying here, in our bed with my Harrison, my head is snuggled on his chest. I can hear the rain on the tin roof, the winds are blowing outside but I can still hear the beating of his heart- and what a kind heart he has.

His arm is wrapped around me-in loving protection which gives me a safe and comfortable feeling. I look at his face which appears so peaceful-he is a very handsome man.

I watch him sleep while thinking how lucky I am to not only be his wife and partner but also his best friend. We have a very close relationship.

Naturally therefore there is loving harmony between us. While in thoughtful reflection during this special moment I see what I have now compared to what I had. I am grateful that he chose me in his life to be his wife, friend, lover and partner.

> **'Let us be grateful to people who make us happy; they are the charming gardeners who make our souls blossom.'**
>
> *Marcel Proust*

CONCLUSION

The information in this book may have you thinking with mixed emotions about the thought of changing. We understand the struggle that can take place in the human mind when being confronted with potentially life changing issues. The idea that in order for a relationship to flourish means coming out of a comfort zone for many.

We understand no one wants their hopes built up then being disappointed over and over again. It is perhaps sometimes hard to trust when you, the reader have gone through much pain or frustration prior to reading this book, but believe me, we both know what that is like.

So, where to from here, you may ask? Is there hope for me? Of course there is. Never think otherwise. Anything in life is worth going for, and it will take the necessary physically, mentally and emotionally effort for decided changes to occur.

Never lose heart. There is no need to be discouraged. In spite of it being a bit difficult to bring these principles outlined into your individual experience and relationship, it will help you be truly fulfilled in ways you have never been before.

It is possible to have love in its truest form. It is possible to have that emotional fulfillment that many have longed for. The sunshine for your heart that we have described in various ways throughout this book can indeed be your reality.

Do you want that? Are you worth it? Personally we believe you are, and that is one of the reasons this book was written.

Our lives and our relationships are definitely not meant to be so cheap and shallow. Our hearts are meant to be filled with sunshine and not darkness. They are meant to be filled with love and not fear.

Our lips are meant to be filled with gratitude and encouragement, not complaining and cursing. So in closing, as you contemplate what has been written within these pages our final thought is to remember that if you always do what you've always done, you will always get what you've always got.

May there forever be sunshine in your heart, like there is in ours

Jordan & Harrison

REFERENCES

Stephen and Alex Kendrick.
The Love Dare Day by Day.
2009. B&H Publishing Group.

Gary Chapman. The five love languages.
1995 Northfield Publishing.

What I didn't learn at school but wish I had'
Jamie McIntyre with Leigh Barker. 2002.

The Ministry of Healing. E.G. White. Pacific Press Publishing Association. 2003. Originally published in 1905

http://www.wiseoldsayings.com/being-thankful-quotes/

http://www.wiseoldsayings.com/keeping-your-head-up-quotes/

https://www.goodreads.com/quotes/tag/peer-pressure

https://www.goodreads.com/quotes/tag/courage

RECOMMENDED READING AND DVDS

Fireproof dvd.
Sherwood Pictures 2008.

The Notebook dvd.
Avery Pix.2004.

Beautiful Dreamer dvd
Wild Horse Production (co-production)
Back Fence Production. (co-production)
2006.

Empowered living. A twelve week plan for improving your most significant relationships
Jim Hohnberger, Tim Canuteson, Julie Canuteson
2002, Pacific Press Publishing Association

The ABC's of Bible Prayer.
Glenn. A Coon. 2001.
Review and Herald Publishing.

Unlocking the champion within.
Mark Bowser, 2007.
Inkstone Press Pty Ltd, Australia.

The Marriage Covenant.
Derek Prince. 1978.

Women who love too much. Robin Norwood.
Arrow Books LTD 1986.

www.ingramcontent.com/pod-product-compliance
Lightning Source LLC
Chambersburg PA
CBHW070506100426
42743CB00010B/1778